TINY ROOM COLORING BOOK

EXPLORE A WORLD OF COSY ROOMS IN THE
TINY ROOM COLORING BOOK

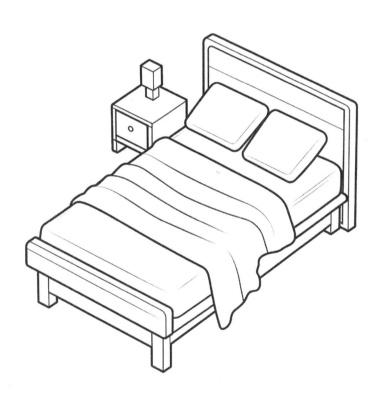

Find More Here:
opqaspace.press@gmail.com

SCAN ME

COLORING TECHNIQUES AND TIPS

WELCOME TO THE POCKET ROOM COLORING BOOK! COLORING CAN BE A DELIGHTFUL EXPERIENCE, AND HERE ARE SOME TIPS AND TRICKS TO MAKE YOUR COLORING JOURNEY EVEN MORE ENJOYABLE:

1. *Start Light:* Begin coloring with a light touch. It's easier to add more color later if needed, but difficult to remove once it's too dark.

2. *Layering:* Experiment with layering colors to create depth and variation. Start with a light layer and gradually add more layers for richer tones.

3. *Sharp Pencils:* Keep your pencils sharp! Sharp pencils allow for precise coloring, especially in smaller areas or detailed sections.

4. *Blending Techniques:* Explore blending techniques such as using a blending stump, tissue paper, or your fingers to blend colors smoothly.

5. *Try Different Strokes:* Vary your coloring strokes - try circular motions, cross-hatching, or back-and-forth strokes to achieve different textures and effects.

6. *Use a Lightbox:* If you want to transfer or trace an image onto another sheet, a lightbox can be helpful for transparency and accuracy.

Best Mediums to Use:

- *Pencils:* Colored pencils are a versatile and popular choice for coloring books. They offer precision, control, and ease of blending.

- *Markers:* Fine-tipped markers can work well, especially for larger areas, but be cautious of bleed-through on thinner paper.

- *Crayons:* Crayons provide vibrant colors but may not offer the same level of precision and blending as pencils.

Remember, the most common and recommended choice for this coloring book is pencils. They allow for detailed work and precise coloring, making your tiny rooms come to life with cozy colors!

Enjoy your coloring adventure in the world of pocket-sized rooms!

COLOR TEST PAGE

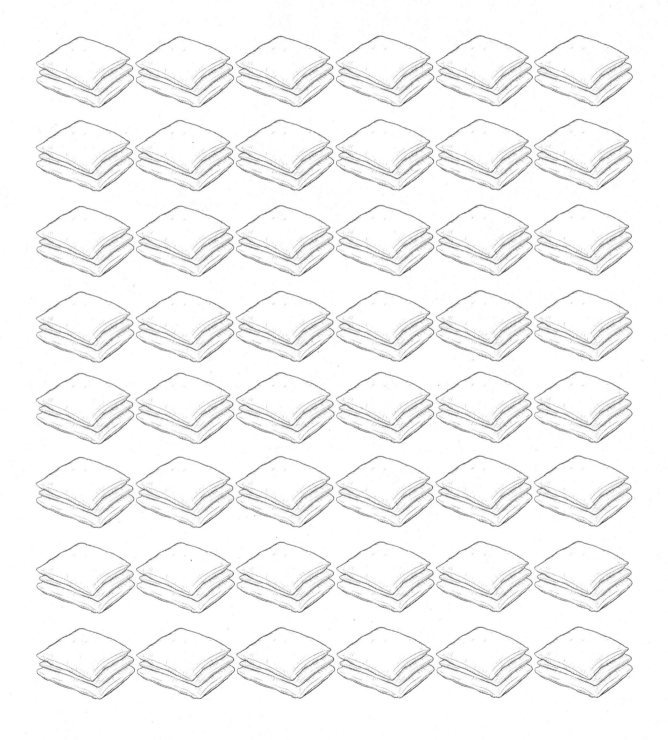

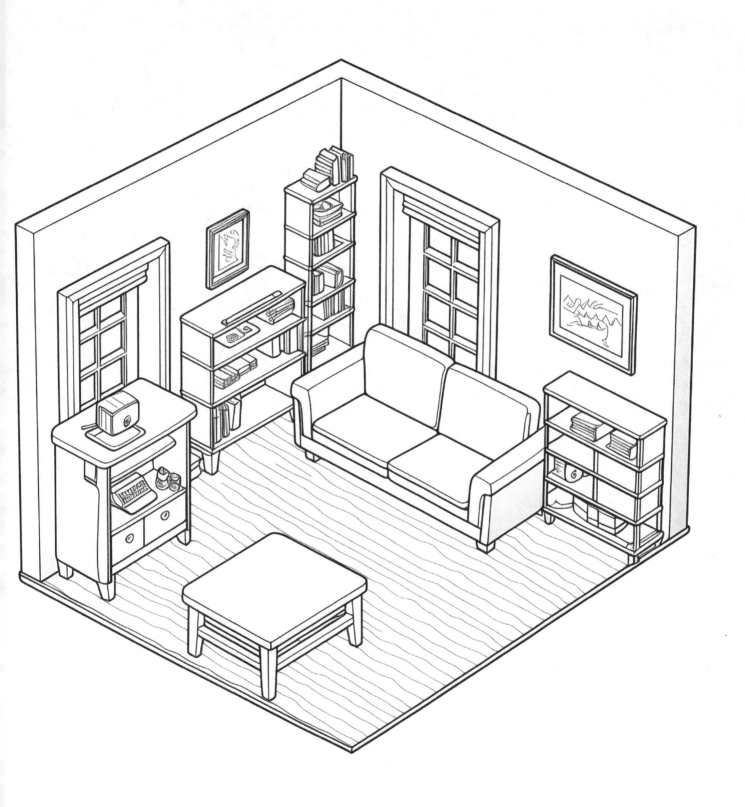

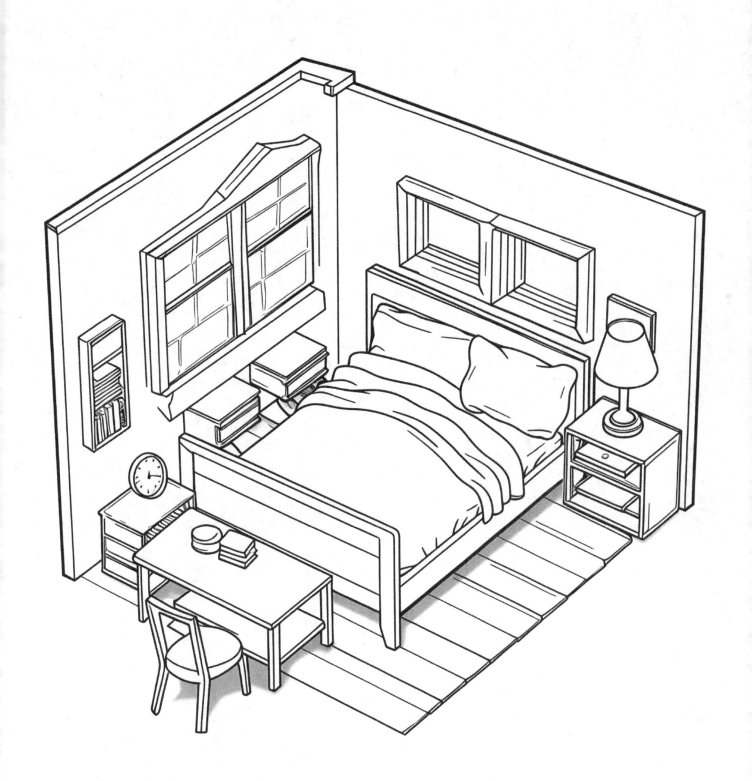

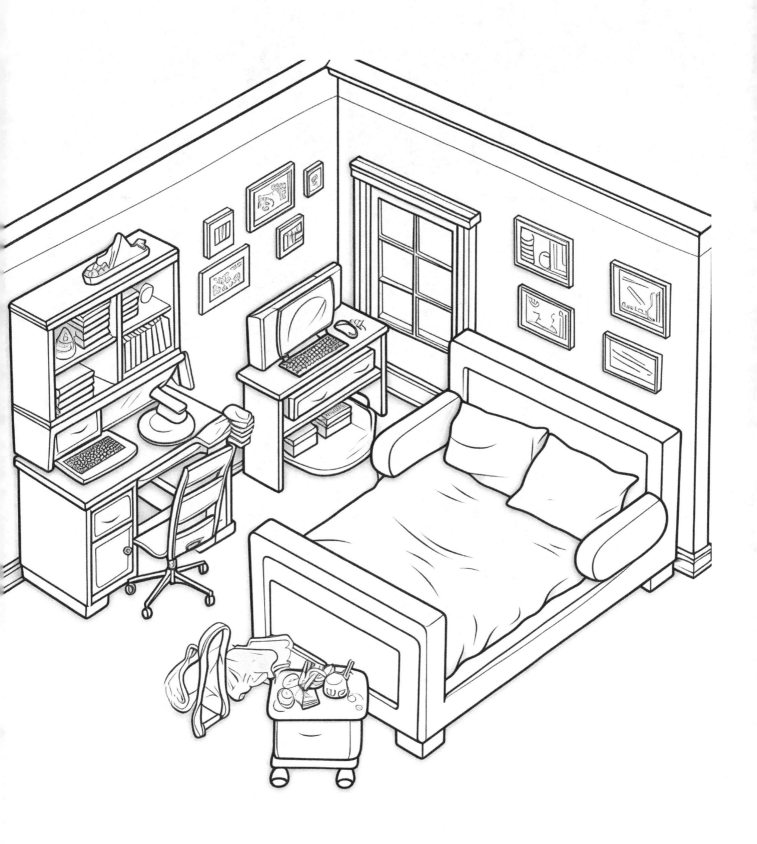

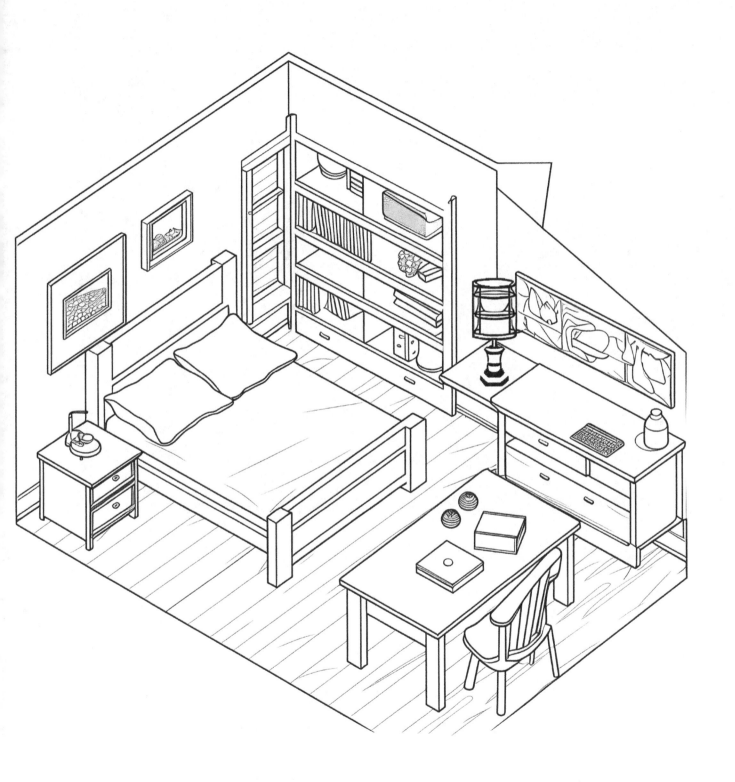

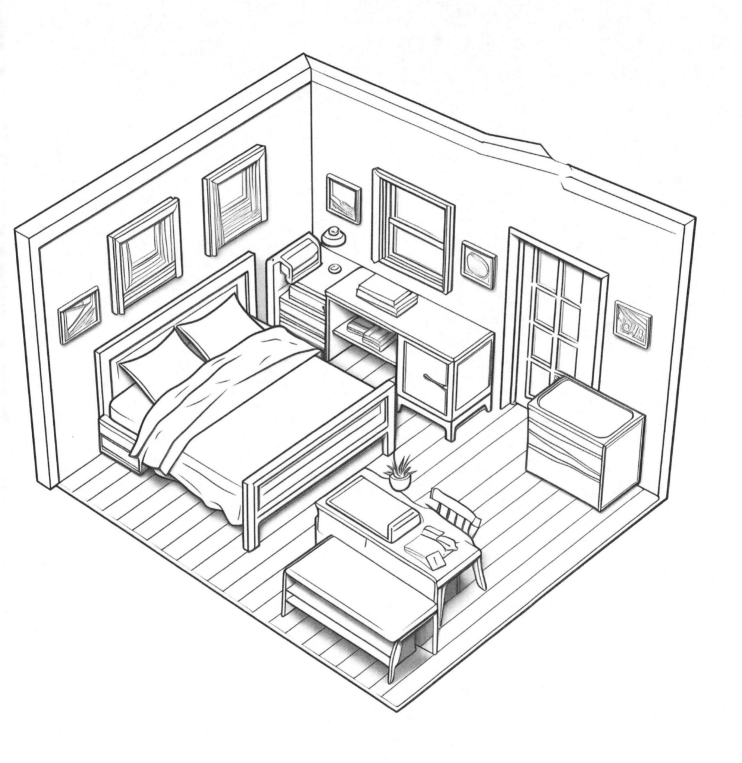

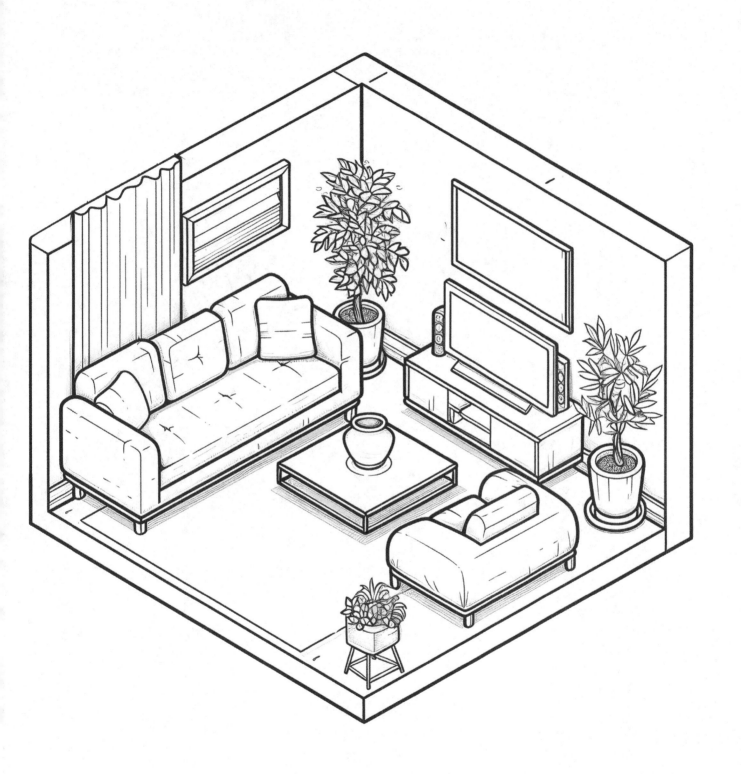

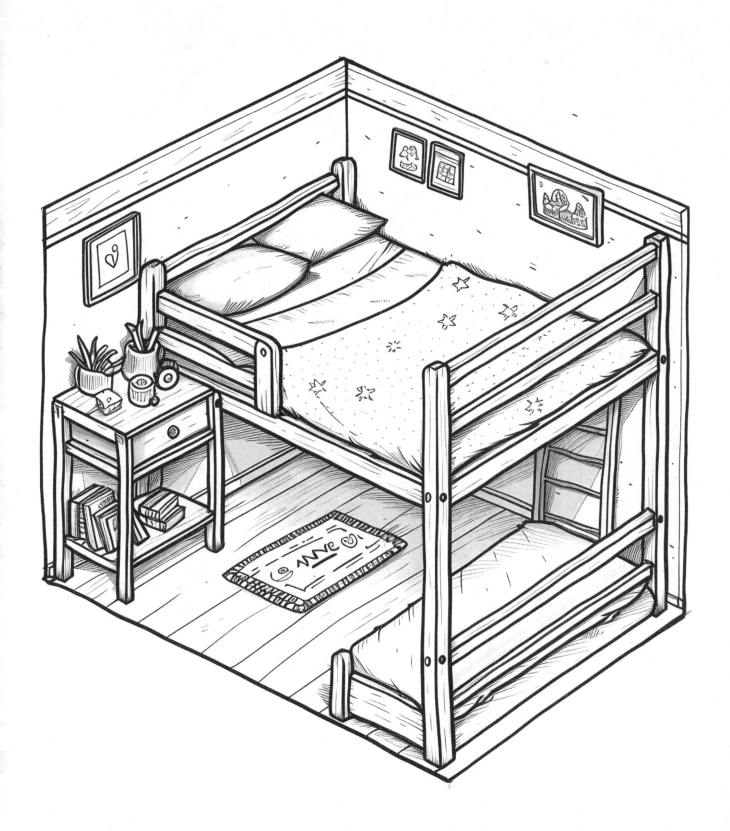

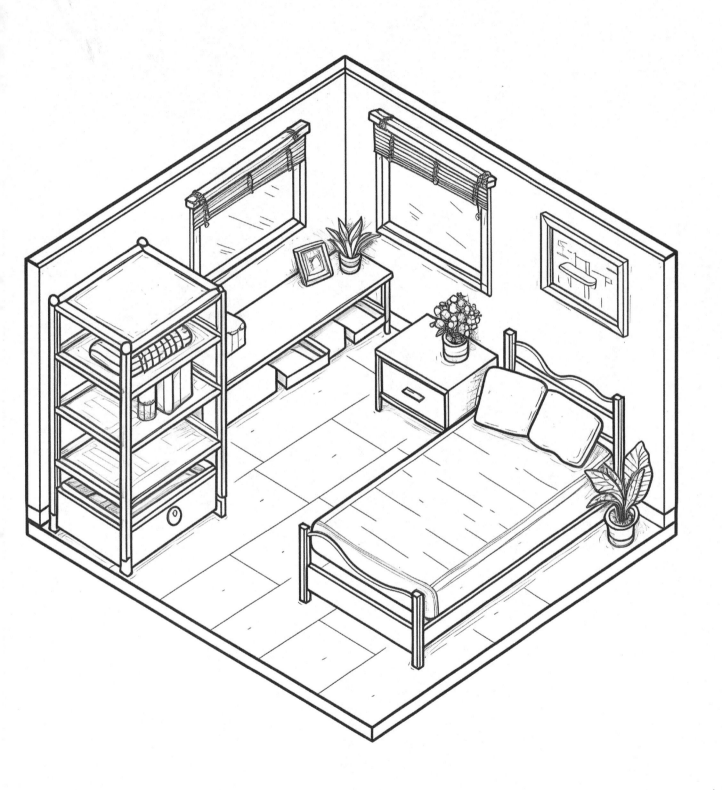

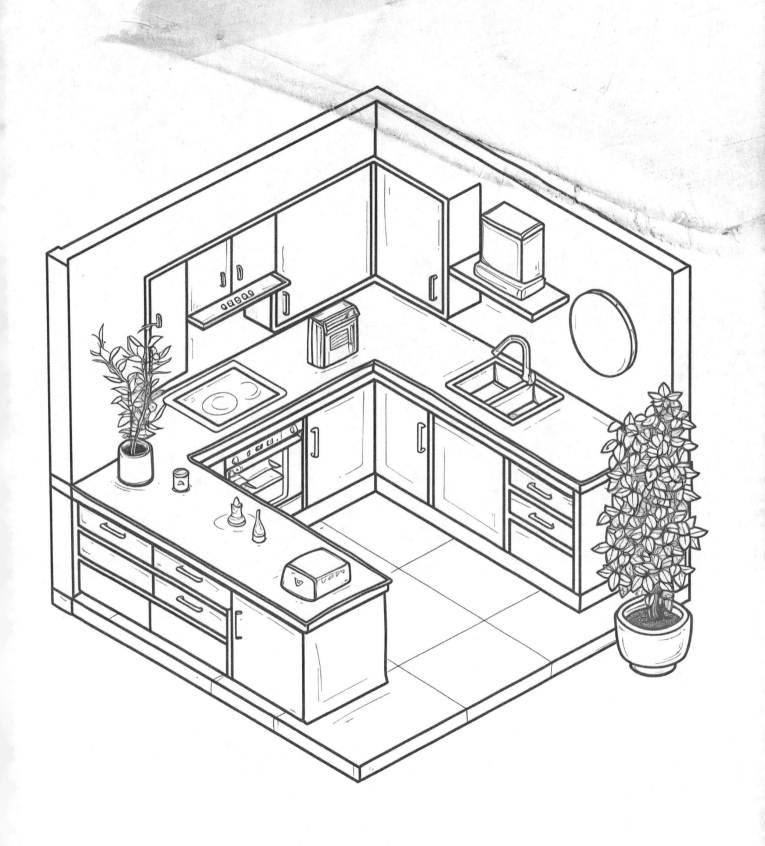

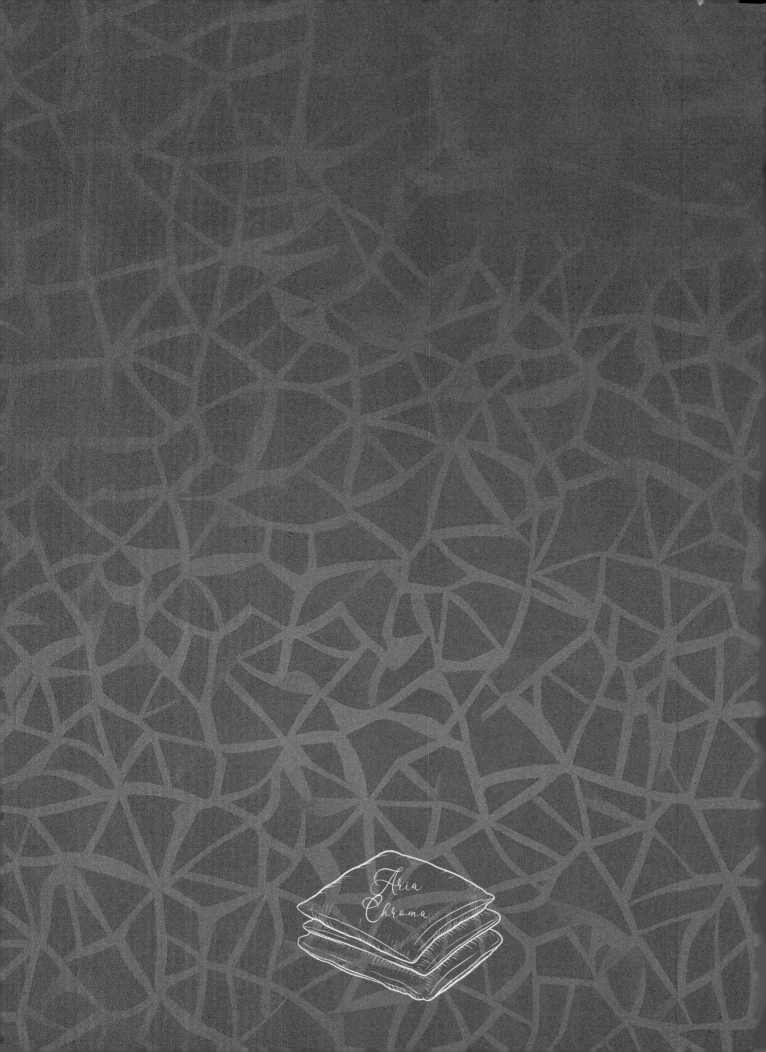

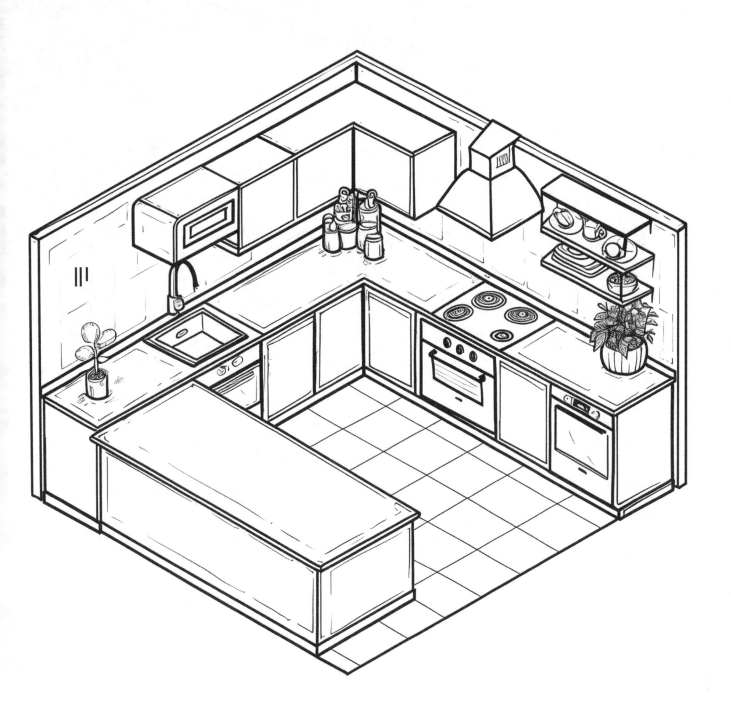

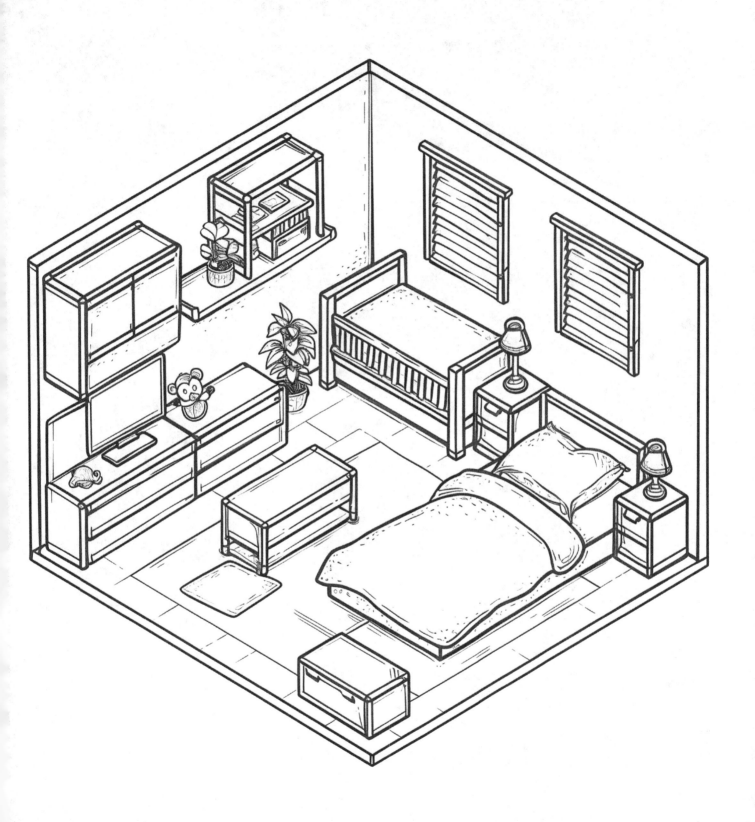

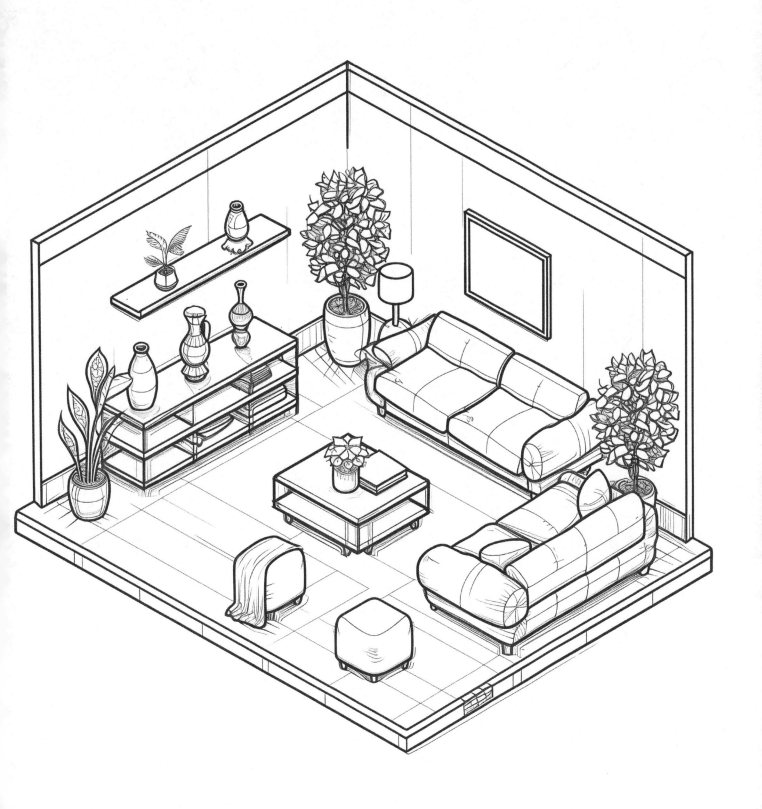

THANK YOU!!

Thank you for being part of this incredible journey through the Tiny Room Coloring Book! Your choice to immerse yourself in these tiny, vibrant worlds means more than just getting a book—it's a shared love for creativity and cozy spaces.

Let your colored rooms stand as a testament to your unique creativity and the joy of making these little spaces your own.

If you've enjoyed coloring these tiny rooms, we'd truly appreciate your support through an honest review on Amazon. Your feedback is what keeps our creative spark alive!

Scan the QR Code

And guess what? As a thank-you gesture, we're thrilled to offer you a free downloadable PDF of the entire book! Yes, you heard it right!
Just reach out to us at opqaspace.press@gmail.com with the subject line "Tiny Room Coloring Book" to unlock your exclusive digital copy. Dive into these delightful spaces and let your imagination run free.

Thank you once again for joining us on this coloring adventure. Claim your bonus now and continue exploring the charming world of pocket-sized rooms at your own pace.

Made in the USA
Coppell, TX
04 April 2025

47916016R00063